Édouard Manet

By Iain Zaczek

WAYLAND

Published in paperback in 2017 by Wayland

Copyright © 2014 Brown Bear Books Ltd.

Wayland, an imprint of Hachette Children's Group
Part of Hodder & Stoughton
Carmelite House
50 Victoria Embankment
London EC4Y 0DZ

Wayland Australia
Level 17/207 Kent Street
Sydney, NSW 2000

Brown Bear Books Ltd.
First Floor
9–17 St. Albans Place
London
N1 0NX

Author: Iain Zaczek
Managing Editor: Tim Cooke
Designer and artwork: Supriya Sahai
Picture Manager: Sophie Mortimer
Design Manager: Keith Davis
Editorial director: Lindsey Lowe
Children's publisher: Anne O'Daly

ISBN–13: 978 1 5263 0034 8

Printed in Malaysia

10 9 8 7 6 5 4 3 2 1

An Hachette UK company
www.hachette.co.uk
www.hachettechildrens.co.uk

Websites

The website addresses (URLs) included in this book were valid at the time of going to press. However, because of the nature of the internet, it is possible that some addresses may have changed, or sites may have changed or closed down since publication. While the author and publisher regret any inconvenience this may cause the readers, no responsibility for any such changes can be accepted by either the author or the publisher.

Picture credits

Key: b = bottom, bgr = background, c = centre, is = insert, l = left, mtg = montage, r = right, t = top.

Special thanks to The Art Archive
Front Cover, ©The Art Archive/Courtauld Institute London/Superstock; All other cover images ©Shutterstock: 4, ©The Art Archive/Kharbine-Tapabor/Coll. S. Kadou; 5tr, ©Shutterstock; 6tl, ©Public Domain/British Library/Etienne Carjat; 6tr, ©Shutterstock/Silvano Audisio; 7, ©Shutterstock/Antonio Abrignani; 8, ©Public Domain/Musée d'Orsay Paris; 9t, ©Public Domain/BHVP/Roger-Viollet; 9b, ©Robert Hunt Library/Robert Lawton; 10-11, ©Public Domain/Alte Nationalgalerie; 11tl, ©Robert Hunt Library; 12-13, ©The Art Archive/National Gallery London/Eileen Tweedy; 14-15, ©The Art Archive/Musse D'Orsay/Dagli Orti; 16-17, ©The Art Archive/Courtauld Institute London/Superstock; 18-19, ©The Art Archive/DeA Picture Library; 21, ©The Art Archive/Musee D'Orsay/Dagli Orti; 22-23, ©The Art Archive/DeA Picture Library; 25, ©The Art Archive/Courtauld Institute London/Superstock/Peter Barritt; 26, ©The Art Archive/Musee d'Orsay/Dagli Orti; 27, ©The Art Archive/Musee d'Orsay/Mondadori Portfolio/Electra.

All artwork: © Brown Bear Books

Brown Bear Books has made every attempt to contact the copyright holder. If you have any information please contact licensing@brownbearbooks.co.uk

Contents

Life story

Édouard Manet came from a respectable background. But in his paintings, he was a rebel who changed the history of art.

Édouard Manet was born in Paris, France, in 1832. His father, Auguste, worked for the French government. He later became a judge. His mother, Eugénie, loved painting. The family thought Édouard would become a lawyer, like his father. But Édouard was more interested in art, like his mother. His uncle, Charles Fournier, took Édouard to look at paintings in the Louvre art gallery in Paris. He also paid for Édouard to have drawing lessons.

Birth name: **Édouard Manet**

Born: **23 January, 1832, Paris, France**

Died: **30 April, 1883, Paris, France**

Nationality: **French**

Field: **Painting, printmaking**

Movement: **Realism, Impressionism**

Influenced by: **Diego Velázquez, Francisco de Goya, Frans Hals, Gustave Courbet**

Édouard Manet, photograph from 1880.

SAILING SHIP In 1848 Édouard got a job as a cabin boy. He sailed to Brazil. He loved Brazil, but he was only there for a short time before his ship sailed back to France.

Auguste refused to let his son become an artist. Instead, he encouraged him to go to sea. Édouard became a cabin boy on a sailing ship. But Édouard was bored at sea. After he failed his exams to become a naval officer, he returned back home.

Now Auguste agreed to let his son train as an artist. Édouard studied with a painter named Thomas Couture. But Édouard also found his training boring. He was a rebel. After six years he had learned to paint in a very traditional way. But what he chose to paint would be very unusual.

Famous Paintings:
- **The Luncheon on the Grass** (1863)
- **Olympia** (1863)
- **A Bar at the Folies-Bergère** (1882)
- **The Execution of Emperor Maximilian** (1869)

'It is not enough to know your craft - you have to have feeling. Science is all very well, but for us imagination is worth far more.'

During his training, Édouard met his girlfriend. She was a piano teacher named Suzanne Leenhoff. They had a baby. Édouard kept Suzanne secret from his father. He and Suzanne did not marry until 1863, after Auguste had died.

Édouard toured Europe. He copied old paintings in art galleries. He liked to copy the style of old Spanish paintings by Velázquez and Goya.

Charles Baudelaire

Édouard's friend Baudelaire was a poet. He believed that poetry could be about modern subjects. His poems were about modern life in Paris.

A new approach

In about 1855 Édouard met Charles Baudelaire. Baudelaire was famous for writing shocking poems. He also wrote about art. He said that artists should paint scenes from modern life. Édouard painted a modern scene, *The Absinthe Drinker*. Édouard sent the picture to the Salon. This was a yearly exhibition of the best paintings in France. But the jury did not let the painting into the exhibition.

History Painting

When Édouard became a painter, most artists painted subjects from ancient history. Myths and bible stories were also popular subjects. This sort of painting was very important to the Salon.

The Salon was an exhibition that showed the best artists and paintings in France. Édouard wanted to do well in the Salon. But he offended people by painting subjects from modern life.

PARIS SALON Every year a jury chose which paintings to exhibit in the Salon. They liked paintings that followed old rules. Édouard and his friends found it difficult to get their paintings accepted.

'The attacks of which I have been the object have broken the spring of life in me ... People don't realise what it feels like to be constantly insulted.'

Starting a scandal

In 1862, Auguste Manet died. He left his son so much money that Édouard could now afford to paint what he liked. The first painting was *The Luncheon on the Grass*. This showed two men having a picnic with a naked woman. The painting was exhibited in a special show. The show was for paintings that had been rejected by the Salon. Édouard's painting caused outrage. In 1865 Édouard painted *Olympia*. It also showed a naked woman. This time the outrage was even greater. Édouard fled to Spain. He soon came home again. He complained that he hated Spanish food.

Important people

Thomas Couture – teacher

Charles Baudelaire – friend, poet

Berthe Morisot – friend, painter

Émile Zola – friend, writer

Berthe Morisot, by Édouard Manet, 1872

Berthe Morisot

Édouard's closest friend among the Impressionists was Berthe Morisot. They met in 1868. Édouard used his friend as a model several times. Morisot often asked for Édouard's advice. In turn, she convinced him to try using lighter colours. She also persuaded him to paint outdoors. In 1874, Berthe married Édouard's brother, Eugène Manet.

This woman's work is exceptional. Too bad she's not a man.

Leader of a movement

By the middle of the 1860s young artists and writers in Paris saw Édouard as the leader of a new modern art style. They thought his paintings were like nothing they had seen before. Édouard spent long evenings talking about art. He talked about ideas with the writer Émile Zola and the artist Claude Monet. The young artists had many ideas for a new way of painting. It would become known as Impressionism.

Off to war

In 1870, France went to war with Prussia (now part of Germany). Édouard became a soldier to help defend Paris. At this time he painted pictures about the sadness of war. He was in Paris when it surrendered to the Prussians in 1871. His studio was destroyed in the fighting.

Things gradually returned to normal. Édouard's friends held an exhibition of their paintings in 1874. Édouard did not take part. He still wanted to be taken seriously by the Paris Salon. But he did take on some of the younger artists' ideas. He tried painting outdoors. This was still a shocking new approach at the time. Artists usually painted in studios.

BARRICADE, PARIS 1871
Édouard was in Paris after the war with Prussia ended. Rebels took over the city for a short time.

'When you've got it, you've got it. When you haven't, you begin again. All the rest is humbug.'

LÉGION D'HONNEUR
Édouard got this honour in 1881. The government gives it to people who play an important part In French life.

Final illness

In 1879 Édouard began to limp. It was the first sign of a sickness called locomotor axia. It became so painful that he found it hard to work. By now his work was being more appreciated. People were used to his style of art. He was finally given a medal at the Salon in 1881. He also got the Légion d'Honneur. But the disease grew worse. Édouard died on 30 April, 1883.

How Manet painted

Édouard liked the art of the past. He wanted to be successful in the traditional art world. But he was also looking for new ways to paint.

Édouard painted new versions of pictures by earlier artists, like the Spanish painter Diego Velázquez. Édouard also took ideas from more modern artists. He was interested in Japanese art. It taught him to paint figures as if they were right next to the viewer.

The Impressionists

The Impressionists had new ideas about art. They wanted to paint things as they really looked. Some people thought their paintings did not look finished. This picture by Claude Monet shows the church of Saint-Germain-l'Auxerrois in Paris in 1867.

PORTE SAINT-MARTIN.

PHOTOGRAPHY
Édouard liked the accidental images he saw in photographs.

Édouard took ideas about how to compose or arrange his subjects from photographs. The camera was still a new invention. Édouard liked the chance images that appear in photographs. Figures may be cut off at the edge. They might be looking at something not shown in the picture. Édouard used these techniques. That means many of his paintings appear to show only a small part of a scene or story.

Édouard was influenced by the Impressionists. Like them, he tried painting outdoors. But he also influenced the Impressionists. They copied his decision to paint modern subjects.

Important Impressionists

Édouard Manet

Claude Monet

Camille Pissarro

Pierre-Auguste Renoir

Mary Cassatt

Berthe Morisot

Alfred Sisley

Music in the Tuileries Gardens

This was one of Édouard's earliest masterpieces. He painted it in 1862. It was his first painting to be noticed by the young Impressionists.

Fashionable people in Paris loved the concerts held each week in the Tuileries Gardens. Édouard often met Charles Baudelaire and other friends there. He made numerous sketches on the spot. Then he painted the picture in the studio. He may have based some of the figures on photographs.

MANET'S

Palette of the picture

This is Édouard's friend, Charles Baudelaire. He helped Édouard choose what subjects to paint.

This tiny patch of sky makes a big difference to the light. If you cover it over, the picture looks much more gloomy.

In the Frame

The original painting of *Music in the Tuileries Gardens* is 76.2 cm (30 in) tall and 118 cm (46.5 in) wide.

Among the crowd are Charles Baudelaire, the composer Jacques Offenbach, and other writers and painters.

Manet liked little jokes. Here, a child's hoop covers part of his signature. This makes it look as if the signature is inside the painting.

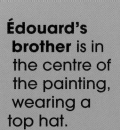

Édouard's brother is in the centre of the painting, wearing a top hat.

Le Déjeuner sur l'Herbe
(The Luncheon on the Grass)

This is the painting that made Édouard famous. He began it in 1862 and finished it the next year. Édouard knew the painting would be shocking to its viewers.

Édouard based the painting on Titian's *Pastoral Concert*, 1576. Clothed men and naked women often appeared in historical paintings. But people were shocked to see them together in a modern picnic scene. The woman was one of Manet's favourite models. Her name was Victorine Meurent. The two men are Édouard's brother and brother-in-law.

In the Frame

The original painting of *Le Déjeuner sur l'Herbe* is 208 cm (81.9 inches) tall and 265.5 cm (104.5 inches) wide.

Édouard also made a smaller, earlier version of the picture.

MANET'S

Palette of the picture

Black is not a colour.

14

Édouard added this bird to his painting. It was not in Titian's painting. The bird is a finch.

The dark woods in the background are painted in a sketchy way.

The food for the picnic is arranged like a still life. Fruit and other food were favourite subjects for painters.

Édouard copied the figures from an older painting. But he did not use the original background. This man seems to be pointing at nothing.

15

A Bar at the Folies-Bergère

This is Édouard's last masterpiece. He painted it in 1882. He was dying from a painful illness. It reminded him of the fun he had had in his life.

Life in modern Paris was Édouard's favourite theme. The Folies-Bergère was a popular club where people went at night. Édouard went there often. This painting was his way of saying goodbye to the life he enjoyed. The woman was a real barmaid. The male customer was Édouard's friend, the artist Gaston Latouche.

In the Frame

🎨 The original painting of *A Bar at the Folies-Bergère* is 96 cm (37.8 inches) tall and 130 cm (51.2 inches) wide.

🎨 The painting originally belonged to the composer Emmanuel Chabrier. He was Manet's neighbour. Chabrier hung the picture above his piano.

Édouard was too sick to paint in the Folies itself. He set up a bar in his studio but painted the rest of the picture from memory.

The Folies-Bergère provided entertainment. These are the legs of an acrobat on a trapeze.

Most of the scene is reflected in a mirror. But they don't look like real reflections. The woman's back would not be visible if we were in front of her.

MANET'S

Palette of the picture

The woman was a real barmaid. Her name was Suzon. She looks bored from standing in a pose in Manet's studio for many hours.

Monet in his Floating Studio

Édouard painted the artist, Claude Monet, at work near Argenteuil in 1874. The town was outside Paris on the River Seine.

The Manet family had a home in the town. The Impressionist painter Monet also lived there from 1871 to 1877. The town was easy to reach from Paris using the new railway system. It was a favourite place for other members of the Impressionist group to visit. Édouard visited Monet there. They painted together outdoors.

Argenteuil was changing quickly. New industries were opening. Édouard shows factory chimneys sending smoke into the sky.

MANET'S

Palette of the picture

In the Frame

🔹 The original painting of *Monet in his Floating Studio* is 82.5 cm (32.5 inches) tall and 105 cm (41.3 inches) wide.

🔹 Manet painted three pictures of boats on the Seine.

Monet's boat had a striped cover. This kept the sun off the painter on hot days.

Monet's wife, Camille, sits in the covered part of the boat. The 'studio' was like a rowing boat with a wooden shed on top.

Monet used his boat as a floating studio. Édouard also painted this picture outdoors. He tried using lighter colours than usual.

Portrait of Émile Zola

Émile Zola was a famous writer. He wrote a piece praising Édouard's paintings. It changed the way people looked at Édouard's work. Édouard thanked Zola by painting his portrait in 1868.

In the portrait, Zola looks as if he is sitting in a writer's study. In fact, the picture was painted in Édouard's studio. Édouard included objects that showed Zola's occupation and personality. Many of the objects belonged to Édouard.

Édouard paints a Japanese print. The screen showing the bird on a branch is also from Japan. These objects show that Zola was also interested in Japanese art.

MANET'S

Palette of the picture

In the Frame

🍃 The original painting *Portrait of Émile Zola* is 146.5 cm (57.7 inches) tall and 114 cm (44.9 inches) wide.

🍃 Édouard painted the portrait as a 'thank you' to Zola. The painting marked the start of a great friendship between the two men.

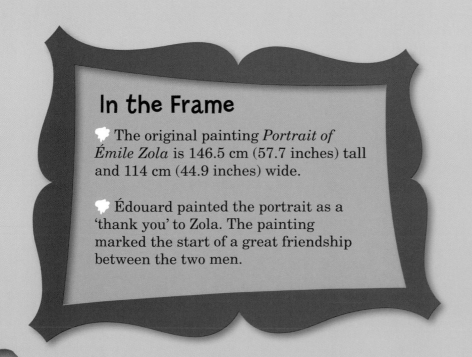

Édouard and Zola both loved Spanish art. This is a painting by the Spanish artist Diego Velázquez.

Manet liked to find new ways to sign his pictures. Here he has put his name on the article Zola wrote about him.

An inkwell and quill pen are included in the picture to show that Zola is a writer.

Gare Saint-Lazare

In 1872 Édouard moved to a new studio. It was near the Gare Saint-Lazare, a railway station in Paris. Several of the Impressionists painted the station and its trains.

The Impressionists saw the railway as a symbol of modern times. Édouard's painting is more mysterious. It does not include a train. It only shows the steam the train has left behind. Édouard shows a glimpse of a woman and child. The woman holds a book, while the girl watches the trains. They are dressed in their best clothes. What are they waiting for? We will never know.

MANET'S

Palette of the picture

This doorway and window belong to Édouard's studio. It was very close to the station.

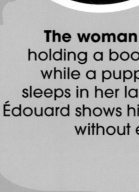

The woman is holding a book, while a puppy sleeps in her lap. Édouard shows hints of a story without explaining it.

This is part of a railway bridge in Paris. The station is a little to the right and does not appear in the painting.

In the Frame

The original painting of *Gare Saint-Lazare* is 93.3 cm (36.7 inches) tall and 111.5 cm (45.1 inches) wide.

The painting is sometimes also known as *The Railway*.

I used short brushstrokes and contrasting colours in my paintings.

The painting is full of odd details, like this bunch of grapes on the wall.

The Banks of the Seine at Argenteuil

This is one of Édouard's most famous 'Impressionist' pictures. He painted it in 1874, during his summer with Claude Monet. That was the year the Impressionists held their first exhibition in Paris.

Édouard was pleased for his friends. But he did not want to join them. He always liked working in his studio more than painting outdoors. He also did not like the Impressionists' quick, unfinished style. He preferred a more careful approach. But Monet persuaded him to try painting outdoors.

MANET'S

Palette of the picture

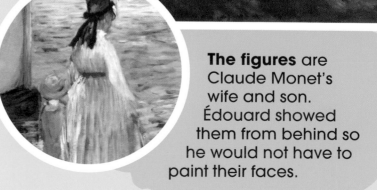

The figures are Claude Monet's wife and son. Édouard showed them from behind so he would not have to paint their faces.

The Impressionists liked painting things that kept changing. Reflections in water were one of their favourite subjects.

In the Frame

The original painting of *The Banks of the Seine at Argenteuil* is 62.3 cm (24.5 inches) tall and 103 cm (40.5 inches) wide.

This was one of Édouard's three paintings of the Seine.

The Impressionists worked quickly and their paintings often lack detail. This hand is just a dab of paint.

The water is painted using short, quick brushstrokes of colour to build up shapes.

What came next?

Édouard was one of the most important painters of the 19th century. He has been called the 'father of Impressionism'.

Édouard Manet's main influence was on the young Impressionists of the early 1860s. They included artists like Claude Monet and Camille Pissarro. These younger painters looked up to Édouard.

His influence was strongest on two artists. One was his friend Berthe Morisot. The other was Edgar Degas.

BERTHE MORISOT was a close friend of Édouard. She also painted pictures that seem to be a snapshot from a story. But the story is never explained.

Berthe Morisot,
Butterfly Hunt, 1874

Edgar Degas, The Gentleman's Race, 1862

DEGAS cut off figures at the edge of the picture, as if they were photographs of a moment in time.

The Impressionists liked Édouard's new approach to art. At the time, most artists painted scenes from history, myth or the Bible. But Édouard painted images from everyday life in Paris. His pictures showed scenes everyone knew, like railway stations. The Impressionists painted similar subjects.

Édouard was criticised a lot for his new approach. But he helped change the kind of subjects artists painted. That is why he is seen as one of the creators of modern art.

How to paint like Manet

It's difficult to paint like Édouard. You can try copying one of his paintings, but you can also have fun making your very own Manet.

WHAT YOU'LL NEED:

- 🖌 some snapshots

- 🖌 a pencil

- 🖌 thick white paper or card

- 🖌 paints

- 🖌 brushes

1.

Choose a photograph that you'd like to copy.

2.

Use a pencil to sketch your picture. Why not choose a picture that only tells part of a story? That will make it mysterious, like some of Édouard's famous paintings.

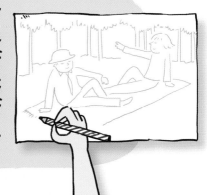

3.

Fill in the main parts of the painting in colour. Think about the shape, not the detail.

4.

Use small brushstrokes. Édouard painted so that different patches of colour were separate, not overlapping.

5.

Add details to the blocks of colour. Add most detail in the most important parts. At the edges of a painting, Édouard often used dabs of paint to suggest the shape of something. There's no need to be exact. Try using a range of colours.

Édouard used colours from deep blacks to bright whites, so his pictures have a lot of contrast.

Timeline

- **1832:** Born in Paris, France.
- **1848:** Becomes a cabin boy on a ship.
- **1850:** Studies art with Thomas Couture.
- **1853:** Travels around Europe to study famous old paintings.
- **1856:** Opens a studio in Paris.
- **1862:** Paints *Music in the Tuileries Gardens*.
- **1863:** Marries Suzanne Leenhoff after the death of his father.
- **1868:** Meets Berthe Morisot, who becomes a close friend.
- **1870:** Joins the National Guard in the war with Prussia.
- **1881:** Receives the Légion d'Honneur.
- **1883:** Dies after an illness.

Glossary

contrast: To be very different from something else.

Impressionist: One of a group of artists who tried to show objects as they appeared at a single glance.

masterpiece: A work of art that shows outstanding skill.

palette: The range of colours an artist uses in a particular painting or group of paintings.

perspective: A technique used in painting to make it seem as if a scene has depth.

portrait: A painting that is intended to show a recognisable person.

pose: A position that someone stands in to be painted or photographed.

print: A picture that is intended to be copied many times.

revolutionary: Something that causes a complete change.

scale: The relative size of things and whether they appear bigger or smaller than each other.

still life: A painting of objects, such as flowers or fruit.

studio: A room where an artist works.

symbol: A sign of something that can't be seen.

traditional: Something that has been done in a certain way for a long time.

Further information

BOOKS

Croton, Guy. *Manet* (The Great Artists and their World). Newforest Press, 2010.

Gunderson, Jessica. *Impressionism* (Movements in Art). Creative Co, 2008.

Mis, Melody M. *Édouard Manet* (Meet the Artist). Powerkids Press, 2007.

National Gallery of Art. *An Eye for Art: Focusing on Great Artists and Their Work.* Chicago Review Press, 2013.

Tracy, Kathleen. Manet (Art Profiles for Kids). Mitchell Lane Publishers, 2008.

MUSEUMS

You can see Édouard's famous paintings from this book in these museums:

Music in the Tuileries Gardens
National Gallery, London, UK.

Le Déjeuner sur l'Herbe
Musée d'Orsay, Paris, France.

A Bar at the Folies-Bergère
The Courtauld Gallery, London, UK.

Monet in His Floating Studio
Neue Pinakothek, Munich, Germany.

Portrait of Émile Zola
Musée d'Orsay, Paris, France.

Gare Saint-Lazare
National Gallery of Art,
Washington DC. USA.

The Banks of the Seine at Argenteuil
The Courtauld Gallery, London, UK.

WEBSITES

www.manetedouard.org
A gallery of all of Manet's paintings.

www.ducksters.com/biography/artists/edouard_manet.php
An illustrated biography on the Ducksters website.

www.theartgallery.com.au/kidsart/learn/manet/
An introduction to Manet from the Worldwide Art Gallery.

Publisher's note to educators and parents: Our editors have carefully reviewed these websites to ensure that they are suitable for students. Many websites change frequently, however, and we cannot guarantee that a site's future contents will continue to meet our high standards of quality and educational value. Be advised that students should be closely supervised whenever they access the Internet.

Index